BRIGHT
IDEA
BOOKS

LAURIE
Hernandez

by Golriz Golkar

CAPSTONE PRESS
a capstone imprint

Bright Idea Books are published by Capstone Press
1710 Roe Crest Drive, North Mankato, Minnesota 56003
www.mycapstone.com

Library of Congress Cataloging-in-Publication Data
Names: Golkar, Golriz, author.
Title: Laurie Hernandez / by Golriz Golkar.
Description: North Mankato, Minnesota : Bright Idea Books are published by
  Capstone Press, [2019] | Series: Influential people | Audience: Grades: 4
  to 6. | Includes bibliographical references and index.
Identifiers: LCCN 2018019502 (print) | LCCN 2018022878 (ebook) | ISBN
  9781543541748 (ebook) | ISBN 9781543541342 (hardcover : alk. paper)
Subjects: LCSH: Hernandez, Laurie, 2000---Juvenile literature. | Women
  gymnasts--United States--Biography--Juvenile literature. | Women Olympic
  athletes--United States--Biography--Juvenile literature. | Olympic Games
  (31st : 2016 : Rio de Janeiro, Brazil)--Juvenile literature.
Classification: LCC GV460.2.H47 (ebook) | LCC GV460.2.H47 L38 2019 (print) |
  DDC 796.44092 [B] --dc23
LC record available at https://lccn.loc.gov/2018019502

Editorial Credits
Editor: Mirella Miller
Designer: Becky Daum
Production Specialist: Megan Ellis

Quote Sources
p. 47, "Laurie Hernandez Reveals the Piece of Advice She Wishes She Knew Sooner." *She Knows*,
October 18, 2017; p. 27, "Laurie Hernandez." *IMDB*, n.d.

Photo Credits
AP Images: Charles Sykes/Invision, cover, Melissa J. Perenson/Cal Sport Media, 12; iStockphoto:
RobMattingley, 30–31; Newscom: Damir Sagolj/Reuters, 6, Kyle Terada/USA Today Sports, 18–19,
Melissa J. Perenson/Cal Sport Media, 8–9; Rex Features: David J. Phillip/AP, 11, 17, Invision/AP,
26–27, Julio Cortez/AP, 23; Shutterstock Images: Kathy Hutchins, 25, Leonard Zhukovsky, 5, 14–15,
20–21, 28

Design Elements: iStockphoto, Red Line Editorial, and Shutterstock Images

TABLE OF CONTENTS

CHAPTER 1

A YOUNG Olympian

The gymnast kept herself steady. Her heart pounded. She caught her breath. She flipped through the air. Boom! She landed on her feet. Then she flashed her big smile.

The crowd cheered. It was a perfect landing! Laurie Hernandez had done well. It was the 2016 Olympic Games. The event was the balance beam. The judges were amazed. She won a silver medal! She hugged her coach. Her dream had come true!

Hernandez's teammates congratulated her on her Olympic performance.

Hernandez smiled after finishing a routine.

6

People loved watching Hernandez. She moved like a dancer. She was always smiling.

Hernandez was only 16 years old at the 2016 Olympic Games. She was the youngest member of the U.S. women's team. She was also **Hispanic**. Few Hispanic gymnasts have become Olympians.

FAVORITE SAYING

Hernandez's favorite saying is "I got this." She says it before she competes.

Hernandez won again before the Olympic Games ended. Her team won a gold medal! It was an exciting time.

Hernandez had worked hard. She had injuries. But she never gave up. She had always wanted to be an Olympic gymnast.

9

CHAPTER 2

AN ATHLETIC Childhood

Laurie Hernandez was born in New Jersey. Her family celebrated their **heritage**. They danced and cooked together. Her parents taught their three kids to be proud of their Hispanic culture.

Hernandez grew up close to her family.

Participating in local gymnastics classes paid off for Hernandez.

ELITE™ 12 PANTENE

Hernandez took ballet lessons when she was five years old. But she was bored. She watched gymnastics on TV. It looked like fun. She wanted to try it. Her parents agreed. She joined a local class.

A BUDDING GYMNAST

As a young child, Hernandez learned moves on the beam. She twisted and twirled. She was a ball of energy. Her coach was impressed. Hernandez learned quickly. She joined a team.

Hernandez performed on the beam.

Hernandez competed at **meets**. Her scores got better. She wanted to become a top gymnast and an Olympian. But she needed higher scores. She trained hard.

CHAPTER 3

CHASING
Her Dream

Hernandez was winning meets at age 9. She was ready for Olympic training. She began training at a camp. She trained for two years. She earned high scores. She had become a top gymnast. But there were tough times ahead.

Hernandez trained hard for the Olympic Trials in Texas in 2015.

Hernandez injured her wrist and knee in 2014. She stopped training. Her body needed to heal. She could not train for one year. But she did not give up. In 2015, Hernandez was ready to compete again. She amazed everyone. She competed in four meets. She won medals at every one!

THE OLYMPIC TRIALS

Hernandez turned 16 in June 2016. She was old enough for the Olympic **Trials**. The timing was perfect. They were in July.

The day of the Olympic Trials arrived. Hernandez's heart raced. She breathed fast. She leaped through the air. She jumped across the beam. She flew from bar to bar. Hernandez placed second overall. Her performance helped her make the team! Her family screamed with joy.

ALL SMILES

Hernandez is known for her bright smile. Her nickname is "the Human Emoji."

Hernandez trained six days a week. It was hard work. But it was worth it. She left the 2016 Olympics as a champion.

Hernandez (center) celebrated with her teammates at the 2016 Olympics.

CHAPTER 4

LIFE AFTER THE Olympics

Hernandez wanted a break from the gym after the Olympics. She wanted to work with kids. She talked to young gymnasts. She visited schools. She encouraged kids to read.

Hernandez wrote a **memoir** in 2017.
I Got This was the title. The book
described her life.

Second grade students listened to Hernandez as she read a story.

A MEDIA STAR

Hernandez danced in a TV competition in 2016. It was called *Dancing with the Stars*. She thrilled the audience. She won!

Hernandez was also in commercials. She talked about Hispanic pride. She wanted to inspire kids. She also talked about nutrition. She wanted kids to eat more healthful foods.

COMPETING AGAIN

Hernandez hopes to compete in the 2020 Olympics.

Hernandez poses with the trophy she won on *Dancing with the Stars.*

25

Hernandez is a great role model. She cares about helping others. She believes in herself. "Embrace every moment," Hernandez once said. "And smile!"

GLOSSARY

heritage
something inherited at birth, such as personal characteristics

Hispanic
of Spanish or Latin American origin

meet
a gathering of athletes for competition

memoir
the story of a person's life as told by themselves

trials
the process of testing or trying out for the Olympics

TIMELINE

2000: Laurie Hernandez is born in New Jersey.

2005: Hernandez takes her first gymnastics class at a local center and meets her current coach.

2009: Hernandez is accepted into the USA Gymnastics development camps for Olympic training.

2014: Hernandez suffers multiple injuries and is forced to stop gymnastics for a year.

2016: Hernandez makes the women's Olympic team. She wins a silver individual medal and a gold team medal.

2017: Hernandez publishes her best-selling memoir, *I Got This: To Gold and Beyond*.

ACTIVITY

ORGANIZE A SPORTS EVENT DAY

Think of a sport you like to play or think you play well. Ask your friends to do the same. With your friends, organize a sports event day. Take turns playing each other's favorite sports. Each person can show the others how to play and give good tips. Make it a fun event like the Olympics. But don't worry about giving scores or competing for medals. Have fun and coach each other instead. Each person can wear a medal for his or her favorite sport!

FURTHER RESOURCES

Inspired by Laurie Hernandez? Learn more about her here:

Lajiness, Katie. *Laurie Hernandez*. Minneapolis, MN: Abdo, 2016.

Time for Kids: A Chat with Laurie Hernandez
https://www.youtube.com/watch?v=Hp1PDZOaz-s

Teen Vogue: 11 Things to Know about Olympic Gymnast Laurie Hernandez
https://www.teenvogue.com/story/11-things-about-olympic-gymnast-
    laurie-hernandez

Find out more about Hernandez's heritage here:

Laurie Hernandez: How My Latina Culture Helped Me Win a Gold Medal
https://www.popsugar.com/latina/Laurie-Hernandez-Hispanic-Heritage-Month-
    Essay-43998199

INDEX